Summary of

Why We Sleep: Unlocking the Power of Sleep and Dreams

Matthew Walker

By Brief Books

Note to readers:

This is an unofficial summary & analysis of *Why We Sleep: Unlocking the Power of Sleep and Dreams,* by Matthew Walker. It is designed to enrich your reading experience.

Table of Contents

Book Summary

Why We Sleep: Unlocking the Power of Sleep and Dreams

Very little has been documented about human sleep habits, until now. If you've ever wondered about the purpose sleep serves in our lives, this is a must read! We know a lot about why and how eating, hydrating, and reproducing are necessities; however, sleep has never been well researched and explained.

Proper rest and sleep allows us to think, learn, make rational and logical decisions. It further resets our emotions, desire to eat and drink, replenishes our immune system and aids our metabolism. Dreaming is our private brand of virtual reality where our brains remember our past, look ahead to our futures and add a good dose of the present to stimulate our creative juices.

With Professor Walker's studies and insights, we'll assess topics like:

- The effects of alcohol and caffeine on our sleep.
- REM and NREM sleep.
- Sleep patterns over time.
- How sleep impacts our health, moods, energy.
- Are sleep aids valuable or harmful?
- Can sleep prevent cancer, diabetes and Alzheimer's?
- Can sleep add years to our life and make us more efficient and successful?

The book is divided into four parts:

- What sleep is and isn't
- The good, the bad and the ugly of sleep
- Dreaming
- Sleep disorders

So, let's get some answers!

Chapter Summary and Analysis

Why We Sleep: Unlocking the Power of Sleep and Dreams

Chapter One

Sleeping less than six or seven hours on a regular basis has several harmful effects on our bodies:

- Immune system breakdown
- Two times greater cancer risks
- Aids in the development of Alzheimer's
- Shortens our life expectancy
- Adversely impacts blood sugar levels
- Increases blocked coronary arteries, which can lead to heart attacks, strokes and heart disease
- Donates to psychiatric conditions like anxiety, depression, and suicide
- Increases the hormone that makes us feel hungry

Because of our neglecting proper sleep times, the World Health Organization has declared a sleep loss epidemic for industrialized nations.

Denying our bodies, the sleep it needs can be fatal for two reasons:

- A rare genetic disorder that begins in midlife when insomnia gets progressively worse, eventually leading to no sleep and the loss of our basic body and brain functions. It is rare; however, scientists surmise that this lack of sleep can cause death.
- Driving while sleep deprived causes thousands of vehicular fatalities, costing not only the life of the sleepless driver but also others involved in the accident. Statistics indicate that one person dies every hour in a sleep-related traffic accident in the United States. That is more than driving while intoxicated or on drugs combined.

Several respected historical figures have tried to analyze the puzzle of sleep including Nobel Prize winner, Francis Crick, Quintilian and Sigmund Freud, all with limited success. Of our four basic drivers, eating, drinking and reproducing, sleep appears to be our most unnecessary need for several reasons:

- We can't gather food, socialize, find a mate and reproduce.
- We can't nurture or protect our children.
- We are most exposed to the dangers of predation.

Sleep is necessary for every species including plants, animals, and humans. The results of this book reveal that sleep is highly relevant to our health as well.

Chapter Two

This chapter focuses on our internal clocks that function on a 24-hour rhythmic pattern, also known as circadian rhythm.
Circadian rhythm is present in all species and sends signals to our brains and all other major organs.

In 1729, Jean-Jacques d'Ortous de Mairan, a French geophysicist tested a plant, the Mimosa pudica. His experiment revealed that the plant's leaves fold at night and display themselves as wilted and in the morning, the leaves re-open to their beauty. The pattern repeats itself every 24 hours, even when the plant is not exposed to sun or light. The plant was placed inside a closed box, yet it's internal clock told it when to open and close proving that even plant life has a circadian rhythm.

In 1938, the next significant sleep discovery was made by Professor Nathaniel Kleitman at the University of Chicago. The professor along with his research assistant, Bruce Richardson took an inventory of food and water that would last six weeks into Kentucky's Mammoth Cave to personally conduct their experiment. They took hospital beds on tall stands to aid in the protection of other cave-dwelling creatures and went so deep into the cavern, one of the deepest known, so that no light was detectable. What they learned was that their circadian rhythm was approximate, rather than precisely, one 24-hour period. The team lasted 32 days in complete darkness and made two breathtaking discoveries:

- Humans, (just like the Mimosa pudica) have natural internal clocks that keep them on a schedule of about nine sleep hours and 15 waking hours.
- Richardson, the younger of the two-gentleman had an estimated 26 to 28-hour clock, and the older Kleitman, experienced a 24-hour clock, both with zero exposure to the visible elements of day and night. Proving that our internal clocks are not precisely set to 24-hour periods.

The result of future studies supports the fact that the human adult has an internal clock of an estimated 24 hours and 15 minutes, very close to the rotation of the earth every 24 hours. While daylight may be the primary method for the resetting of our internal clocks, our brains also respond to additional cues, like exercise, food, temperature changes and social interactions. This biological clock is called, suprachiasmatic nucleus, and is in the middle of our brain where it can detect light via our optic nerves to reset our internal clocks.

No matter the outside conditions, our natural body temperatures begin a slow rise around noon and into the early afternoon. In the afternoon, our temperatures begin to decline and continue doing so through about three to four in the morning, when it begins a slow rise. And, those facts don't change even if we have a sleepless night, proving again, that our bodies are controlled by the circadian rhythm. We've all likely defined ourselves, or have been defined as morning larks or night owls, and the difference is well known and very clear. However, if you force one or the other to abide by the opposite schedule, it creates a bit of chaos and discomfort, as well as less efficient thinking. Essentially, forcing someone to be what they are not wired to be, on a consistent basis, can lead to higher rates or poor mental and physical health. Genetics largely determine our chronotype (morning or night people).

The hormone, Melatonin, also known as the "hormone of darkness," kicks in at night time and tells our body it's time to rest. It doesn't play any other role in our sleep, other than to tell us it's bedtime. It is worthy of note that some of us take Melatonin supplements as sleep aids and it is not a hormone supplement that is monitored by the Food and Drug Administration (FDA). What that means is that when you make a purchase, the listed concentrations of Melatonin can vary by as much as 83 percent less or 478 percent more than is disclosed. Our bodies know to stop further release of Melatonin in the morning, so we know it's time to get our day started. Graphically, this would be displayed as an even line across the day, with a huge increase between the hours of about 9 pm to 6 am, with the peak around 1 am.

This helps us to understand better jet-lag, as well as the inclination to struggle more as we travel to the east over flying towards the west. Eastbound dictates you fall asleep earlier than normal, which is usually more difficult than traveling to the west, which requires us to stay up later. Research studies have been performed on flight staffs who frequently fly longer routes, with little or no opportunity to recover their "normal" wake and sleep times. Two findings were identified:

- Parts of the brain had physically shrunk, indicating a loss of brain cells.
- Short-term memory was impaired.

Perhaps more bothersome, they had higher propensities to develop cancer and type 2 diabetes than the public.

Melatonin and our circadian rhythm are only the first factors that determine wake versus sleep. The second is called sleep pressure. Adenosine develops in our brains the entire time we are awake and as it increases it encourages us to sleep, most commonly after 12 to 16 waking hours. Caffeine is the "anti-adenosine," and it can negate the absorption of adenosine in our brain receptors. What you may not realize is the fact that caffeine stays alive in our bodies longer than you might think. Its average life is about five to seven hours. So, if you are prone to a cup of joe after dinner, it could have an adverse impact on the urge to sleep, as well as the quality of sleep. Also, be aware that de-caffeinated drinks still have caffeine in reduced amounts, generally 15 to 30 percent of a regular cup of coffee. That said, some people, for genetic reasons, can dispose of caffeine more quickly. As we age, our natural ability to clear caffeine from our bodies tends to slow, so that late cup of coffee could be something you want to reconsider. Once the caffeine clears via our liver, some people experience a caffeine crash and are overcome with sleepiness.

Chapter Three

How do you recognize when someone is sleeping? There are three primary ways:

- Our stereotypical position, horizontal.
- Because our muscles are at rest, we tend to assume a bit of a slumped position, fully supported by whatever in under us (the bed, couch or chair).
- A lack of responsiveness.

How do you know that you have slept?

- You lost consciousness and any perception of the outside world.
- You lose your conscious sense of time.

Researchers have recorded our sleep signals in three ways:

- Brainwave actions.
- Eye movements.
- Muscular activities.

In 1952, Eugene Aserinsky, a University of Chicago graduate student, studied eye movements during both walking and sleeping hours. He partnered with our Mammoth Cave participant, Professor Nathaniel Kleitman, to learn that there are periods of time during sleep that our eyes will quickly move from left to right. After some time, our eyes returned to a calm and motionless state, but the pattern repeated itself over the course of a normal sleeping period, typically every hour and a half. This was the birth of REM (rapid eye movement) and NREM (non-rapid eye movement). NREM can be broken down further into four stages defined by the degree of difficulty of waking the sleep candidate. While we begin our sleep with a prolonged NREM state, the later half of our rest has more REM sleep or dreaming opportunities. Our NREM sleep time is spent sorting our unneeded neural connections and REM comes in later to strengthen the remaining connections. Graphically, REM sleep closely mirrors our awake brain waves. In fact, in REM sleep, our brains can be as much as 30 percent more active than our awake hours. NREM significantly varies to a far more spastic picture with constant ups and downs.

Another interesting finding is that seconds before we fall into REM sleep, our bodies become paralyzed for the duration of REM. Of course, our involuntary muscles allowing us to breath remain intact. Think of it as our sleep time seat belt, keeping us motionless. With age, can also come a reduced ability to control our dream enhanced motor skills, so you may see someone elderly, physically acting out a dream.

Chapter Four

Research has further revealed that all life forms, everything from worms to plants, to humans and animals and even to bacteria, all have some circadian rhythm, based on our light to dark natural cycles. What this tells us is that the art of sleep has been with us for at least 500 million years. You may be asking yourself, "why did anything bother to wake up?"

Two theories have been discussed related to this phenomenon:

- Sleep was the first state of life and wakefulness followed. Wakefulness is certainly the more potentially damaging condition for all lifeforms.
- Sleep is needed to allow us to recover from any damage done during our awake hours.

While sleep is a consistent commonality between all creatures in the animal kingdom, there are four differentiators:

- The total amount of sleep time needed.
- Elephants only sleep about four hours each day.
- Big cats, sleep 15 hours per day.
- Brown bats sleep 19 hours a day.

It is believed that this is caused by several factors relating to diet, location on the food chain, social network, metabolic rate, and complexity of the nervous system. Not all species experience the same sleep stages of REM and NREM. Our aquatic friends, do not consistently experience any REM sleep.

The third difference is how we sleep. Again, water creatures only sleep with one half of their brain, so that the other half can stay alert to predators. Birds operate similarly, by sleeping with half a brain and one eye always open for predators. However, if the birds are in the group, they line up and rotate guard duty.

- The fourth variant is pressure. The US Government considers this a matter of national security because a sleep-deprived person can weaken quickly and be more apt to disclose secrets. The need for sustenance or protection will come ahead of sleep in all animals, including humans.

The question of how we should sleep has two answers. First, in the industrialized nations, we tend to sleep monophasically, or we get all our sleep at one time, generally at night. In more remote areas that may not have our luxuries or even electricity, they tend to sleep at night and rest for 30 minutes to an hour during the day. These "napping communities" tend to live as much as four times longer than an individual in an industrialized nation.

Another variant for humans is that we sleep less than any other primates. Our sleep is about 20 to 25 percent REM and our total sleep time is about eight hours. In contrast, other primates sleep ten to 15 hours per night and only nine percent of that time is spent in REM phase. Our author credits this fact to two primary things:

- Our level of social intricacy.
- Our superior intelligence (as compared to other primates).

Remember that human REM sleep also allows us to control our emotions, be creative, socialize appropriately, and think rationally.

Chapter Five

Our sleep habits begin in utero, when we spend an estimated six hours in REM, another six hours in NREM and the remaining twelve in a type of sleep that can't be defined as either category. By the last trimester, our sleep time has decreased; however, since REM sleep is required to ensure a maturing brain, we increase that type of sleep to about nine hours.

It takes an average of three to four months for the infant to begin developing a more customary sleep pattern and by about one year of age, they have adopted a sleep schedule more akin to that of the parents (with the addition of naps).

- One other thing that changes from infancy into early and late childhood is the proportion of REM and NREM sleep.
- An infant will have a 50/50 split.
- A five-year-old is more of a 70/30 split (NREM/REM).
- The proportion of REM sleep decrease as the child ages; however, by early teenage years, the balance stabilizes to what most adults are accustomed to, and 80/20 split.
- The circadian rhythm changes as we grow from infancy into our teens, which is why younger children will be ready for an earlier bedtime and teenagers are more likely to stay up later. To put this in a clearer perspective, asking your teen to make a 10 pm bedtime is akin to asking the parent to go to bed at 7 pm because the teen's circadian rhythm is still developing into a stable condition.

Alcohol is known to be one of the strongest suppressants to REM sleep, just one of the reasons expectant mothers should not drink during pregnancy. While it's not a cause of autism, there is a correlation between the two in that children diagnosed as autistic have a common thread of disruptive sleep. Alcohol use during pregnancy is known to lead to a greater propensity for a child to have autism.

The next large research effort came from a pioneer in the sleep business, Irwin Feinberg. He concluded that downscaling of REM sleep in early teens happens because the brain is less rational at that time of life. Also, the individuals usually exhibit poor decision-making skills, and they take greater risks. During his ten-year study, he collected over 3,500 all night assessments and more than 320,000 hours of recorded sleep. As our deep NREM sleep lessens in intensity, thinking skills, and reasoning begins to improve, and the brain is naturally guiding us into adulthood. So, the inference now is that deep NREM sleep plays a more significant role in brain maturing than originally believed. Further, the sleep intensity begins in the back of our brains and moves to the front, which is why reasoning skills are the last to develop. So, when you ask your teenager, "What were you thinking?" the answer is likely that they weren't, at least not yet!

That said, a couple of teenage risks exists at this juncture. Not getting the right amount of both NREM and REM sleep has been linked to a propensity to develop schizophrenia in teens and young adults. The second issue is early school starting times, which may cause a shift in their circadian rhythms.

Research regarding the role that sleep plays in our development is continuing, and more learning opportunities exist.

As we age into our senior years, sleep is still a very necessary element; however, for three reasons, we may not be getting the sleep we still need. Because:

- The quantity and quality of sleep have changed. Our health has also likely changed, and we may be taking additional medications that can be disruptive to our circadian rhythm. Medical professionals may be so focused on the medical condition treatment and fail to consider the changes in sleep habits. Changes in our brains also contribute to changes in our REM and NREM sleep timings and proportions, which is also disruptive. The portion of our brains that controls our circadian rhythm is also the part that tends to suffer earliest as we age.
- Our sleep is less efficient. Our melatonin production decreases, which encourages an earlier bedtime. This is the reason for earlier dinner times for seniors, particularly in retirement communities. As seniors,

we compensate for this change by rising earlier in the morning as well.

- Our sleep timing has changed. As we get older, we tend to wake up more during the night for an assortment of reasons, which creates fragmentation in our sleep time and disturbs and REM and NREM sleep times.

Efforts are underway in the healthcare industry to provides aids for seniors to address the sleep changes to ensure they do not continue having such an adverse impact on our retirement years.

Chapter Six

The benefits associated with proper sleep have been researched and documented in more than 17,000 scientific reports. The benefits include:

- Longer life
- Enhances creativity
- Improves memory
- More physically attractive
- Fewer food cravings and slimmer
- Protects from cancer and dementia
- Aids in prevention of colds and flu
- Lowers the risk of heart disease, stroke, and diabetes
- Feel happier, less anxious and less depressed

Our brains have a defined amount of short-term memory storage capacity called a hippocampus, and when we run out of room, it starts overwriting older memories, much like a computer would overwrite older documents. To study this storage, a team did a test with two groups of healthy adults. Each participant was shown 100 pairs of faces and was later asked to repeat them back to the research team. Both groups performed comparably. After that, one group took a 90-minute nap, while the second group surfed the net or played games and stayed awake. By 6 pm the same day, both groups were shown a different set of 100 pairs of faces, the group who had the nap performed significantly better, to the tune of 20 percent better than the group who stayed awake. The nap helped to restore the memory capacity. These findings have been replicated in numerous other studies. However, for older adults, age 60 to 80, sleep did not produce the same results, which again points to the need for non-pharmaceutical methods to address and improve sleep for older individuals.

A study performed in 1924 by John Jenkins and al Dallenbach pitted sleep versus awake to determine its memory impact. All participants were verbally given a list of facts and then asked to repeat them back at intervals over an eight-hour awake period and across a full night of sleep. As you might expect, sleep time helped to make the memory firmer, while awake time made the storage of memories more forgettable. It wasn't until studies were performed in the 1950s that we began to learn more about how sleep aided memory retention. Studies in the early 2000s further substantiated the same results.

Technology is allowing for studies to be performed on varying methods for aiding our sleep brain waves, and they include some promising opportunities such as:

- Playing tones over speakers near the bed
- Gently rocking the bed from side to side (with the bed being raised from the floor)

Now consider memories we may want to forget. They may be painful and when remembered places you back at a time that was sad, painful or threatening in some way. Not only do we want to forget this memory, but we can also free up some storage space in our brains by letting it go. In 1983, Frances Crick, a Nobel Laureate recipient did some studies that suggested that our REM sleep acts in a way that removes unwanted or overlapping memories. At the time, it was just a thought, and it wasn't until 2009 that our author and his graduate assistant tested Mr. Crick's idea. Their test showed all participants a listing of works, followed by the letters, "R" (for remember) or "F" (for forget). As in earlier tests, after the displayed words were shown, half of the participants were given a 90-minute nap, while the remaining cast stayed awake. At 6 pm on the same day, both groups were asked to remember as many words as they could, regardless of the direction to remember or forget. The overwhelming result was that sleep significantly improved the memory of words that were to be remembered, yet it did nothing to the memory of the words the group was instructed to forget. What this tells us is that sleep is even more powerful than originally known, it's also smart, and can pick and choose what it wants to remember. Also, in conflict with Mr. Crick's results, all this happened during NREM sleep, rather than REM.

Studies of this nature will continue so we may learn how to harness and control those memories better. To this point, we have only reported on factual memory. Let's look at muscle memory abilities.

First and foremost, muscles do not have memories; those memories are tied to our brains, which is where the memory is stored and retained. That led to the next question our author had, which was how does it happen, that we can go to bed frustrated with our motor skills (or lack thereof). That we can't learn or remember "X," yet in the morning, it's all clear? Is the answer: time, time asleep or time awake? Again, as in earlier similar tests, participants were asked to practice typing a sequence of five numbers. They all practiced and improved in both speed and accuracy. Twelve awake hours later, half of the participants have tested again and shown no improvement in their typing of those same five numeric characters. The remaining half slept for an estimated eight hours overnight and were re-tested the following morning. As you should now expect, the results were that the group who had the overnight rest period improved their accuracy and speed by 35 and 20 percent respectively. Also, the group who remained awake was later provided another testing opportunity after they had time for eight hours of rest, and the results were the same as the participants who had rested earlier. What this tells us is that the brain will allow for improved motor skill improvement, even without additional practice. We're not implying that practice can be eliminated though. Another important outcome was the fact that nothing moved to short or long-term memory banks, rather the motor skills were stored in brain circuits that live below our conscious level. Which means, they had become instinctual, nearly without thought or effort. Today, sports teams, including Olympians have built naps into their training routines and before performance time because they have recognized what we've learned in these continuing studies. Getting less than six to eight hours of sleep nightly can result in as much as a 30 percent drop to exhaustion, and the effort your heart puts out is also reduced. Sleep also helps to reduce the risks of a sports injury.

This is also good news for stroke victims because again, sleep will help their brains rebuild the connections to help them recover from the effects of a stroke.

Chapter Seven

We have already learned that sleep deprivation has highly critical adverse impacts up to and including death. However, the following questions remain:

- How long can a human remain awake and not have their performance adversely impacted?
- How much sleep can we lose over a period of nights before our brain fails to process critical functions?
- How many nights of recovery sleep does it take to restore normal performance after a loss of sleep?

To learn the answers to these questions, Professor David Dinges at the University of Pennsylvania had participants perform a simple task (pushing a button every time a light came on in a confined boxed area) for ten consecutive minutes every day for a period if 14 days. Participants were in a controlled lab environment, and each person started out with a full eight-hour opportunity for sleep the night before commencing the test. After each was tested, the group divided into four groups; each one provided different amounts of sleep deprivation:

- The first group was up for 72 straight hours.
- The second group was limited to four hours of sleep each night.
- The third group received six hours of nightly sleep.
- The fourth and final group was allowed a full eight hours of sleep each night.

Some of the results were expected:

- Reaction time slowed in all four groups, in some cases there was no response at all.
- Those who slept an eight-hour night maintained a stable, nearly perfect performance for the full 14 days.
- The group who stayed up for a full 72 hours performed horribly. Their concentration levels decreased by more

than 400 percent. Performance worsened each of the 14 days with no signs of leveling out.

- The group that had only four hours of sleep performed as bad as the team who had not slept for 24 hours straight and over time; performance continued to degrade throughout the testing period.
- The most surprising group, who got six hours of sleep per night (what most of us get each night), took just ten days to perform as poorly as those who had been deprived of sleep for 24 hours. Again, there were no signs of the degrading performance leveling out to a flat line.

Other similar studies corroborate these findings. Also, and perhaps equally disturbing is that sleep-deprived people don't know when they are deprived. As a result, they don't know to take added precautions. Other tests report that being sleep deprived behind the wheel of a car is equally as dangerous as being legally drunk. To answer our questions from the beginning of this chapter:

- How long can a human remain awake and not have their performance adversely impacted? Sixteen hours
- How much sleep can we lose over a period of nights before our brain fails to process critical functions? After ten nights of only seven hours of sleep, our brains are as impaired as they would be if we had gone a full 24 hours without sleep.
- How many nights of recovery sleep does it take to restore normal performance after a loss of sleep? Three full nights of sleep are still not enough to bring us back to "normal" after a week's worth of short sleeping.

The key take-away from this chapter: if you haven't slept well for an extended period, or if you feel drowsy, stop driving and sleep! Studies have consistently proven that nothing can restore our brain's critical functions better than sleep. That includes caffeine, drugs, and naps!

During similar testing for how emotions are impacted by sleep deprivation, results tell us that emotional reactions are then 60 percent escalated in sleep-deprived individuals. Our emotions are triggers by our amygdala, which lies on both the right and left sides of our brains and is also responsible for our "fight or flight" responses.

The chapter concludes with reiteration regarding the contributions that a lack of sleep makes to mental disorders as well as Alzheimer's.

Chapter Eight

Sleep deprivation also impacts other areas of our health. In fact, sleep touches every nook and cranny of our bodies.

Cardiovascular impacts:

- One study showed that people who routinely get six or fewer hours of sleep per night are four to five hundred percent more likely to face heart attacks. Adults 45 years or older who sleep fewer than six hours per night are 200 percent more likely to suffer a stroke or heart attack. Just missing one or two hours per night will speed up our heart rate, which will result in increased blood pressure.
- A lack of sleep also adds strain to our blood vessels, leaving them more susceptible to blockages and narrowing We all have "sympathetic" nervous systems, which helps to guide our fight or flight response stress, and a lack of sleep makes our nervous system more active, which increases the strain on our heart and blood pressure. Because sleep deprivation adversely impacts our growth hormones, which replenish out blood vessels, they begin the process of losing their integrity.

Diabetes and weight gain impacts:

- An initial study showed that participants who had limited sleeping time were 40 percent less able to absorb glucose that was being absorbed when they were getting a full eight hours of sleep per night. A lack of sleep also hampered the concentration levels of leptin and ghrelin, which are our signals to feel satisfied from hunger, so we feel hungry.
- And it isn't necessarily the number of calories we consume; it's the quality of the calories. Studies had shown that when sleep deprived, we tend to hunt for less healthy snack foods (cookies, chips, candy and other carb-heavy foods). Interestingly, a lack of sleep also

increases endocannabinoids (yes, that is related to cannabis), and it stimulates our appetite. Or more appropriately, gives us the munchies. The obesity epidemic in our county can at least partially be related to our tendency to get less than eight hours of sleep per night. The other amazing finding, a lack of sleep causes us to lose lean body mass, or muscle, not fat.

Reproductive system impacts:

- For men, a lack of sleep leads to a decreased level of testosterone, which has the effect of aging men by as much as 15 years regarding virility. For women, the same lack of sleep causes about a 20 percent drop in follicular releasing hormone, which is released before ovulation and is key to reproduction.
- A lack of sleep has also been proven to make us all look less attractive. Several studies have been performed where people from the public made a judgment on participants who have slept a full eight hours versus those who slept less, and the consensus was that the subjects who slept less, physically looked more tired, less healthy and less attractive.

Immune system impacts:

- Sleep is a known warrior that fights infection and illness. Studies have proven that for those of us who get routinely less sleep are nearly 50 percent more apt to catch colds and the flu.
- Sadly, this condition holds true for our cancer-fighting immune cells as well. Remember that our sympathetic nervous system gets revved up when we lose sleep, which triggers inflammation and can lead to many health problems, including issues related to cancer. If, or when cancer rears its ugly face, poor sleep acts as a fertilizer and enhances growth.

Genes and DNA impacts:

- A lack of sleep alters our genetic makeup by interfering with the chromosomes. More specifically, the protector (called a telomere) that helps avoid any chromosome damage. Yes, a lack of sleep can change you and your essence.

Chapter Nine

When we dream, we become just a little psychotic, but don't worry yet! It's perfectly normal!

- We hallucinate
- We become delusional
- We get disoriented
- Our emotions go from one end of the spectrum all the way to the opposite end (aka affectively labile)
- Once awake, we suffer from amnesia

In our waking lives, this would be a bit disconcerting, but in dreamland, it's all good! Sigmund Freud, many moons ago, made the non-scientific statement that dreams were a form of wish fulfillment. And that theory has been the standard approach for 100+ years. While Dr. Freud's opinion had significant and correct virtues, it also has some flaws.

Why do we dream? We already know that most of our dreaming takes place during REM sleep and we know the value and necessity of REM sleep. Thanks to technological advances, during an MRI scan, we can see that once we transition from NREM to REM sleep, parts of our brain light up, literally on the scan. Specifically, the lit areas are:

- In the back of the brain, our visuospatial region, which enables our visual perceptions.
- Movement control, motor cortex.
- Remember the hippocampus, which supports our autobiographical memory.
- Our brain's emotional centers: the amygdala and the cingulate cortex.

Each region shows as much as 30 percent more activity in REM sleep than in awake times.

The next logical question was: "Can we predict the content of dreams?" The short answer is yes. A team of Japanese scientists performed numerous tests with the aid of MRI scans and dream summaries from participants. What they learned was surprising! They were able to use the MRI data to determine what the dreamers saw in their dream. While the method is not yet perfected, it is promising. That said, it could present an ethical conundrum: does anyone else need to know the contents of our dreams?

On the subject of dream content several beliefs have existed:

- The Egyptians and the Greeks believed that dreams were sent from the Gods.
- Aristotle believed that dreams were simply originated in our minds from waking events.
- Freud, as we noted earlier believed that dreams were wished fulfillment.

Freud was close when he noted that dreamers had a protective device that took repressed wishes, and disguised them in our dreams. Since science was never able to prove the good doctor wrong or right, Freud's beliefs have dominated psychoanalytic practices. Today, based on volumes of dream reports, we know that the day's events are only found in about one to two percent of dreamers, and they are not a replay of our waking thoughts. As much as 55 percent of our dreams can mirror our emotions from the day.

Chapter Ten

You may be wondering now, what purpose dreams serve in our lives, or if they are just a byproduct of REM sleep. The answer is that they do indeed serve a valuable purpose, they:

- Aid our mental and emotional health.
- Enhance our problem-solving skills.
- Make us more creative thinkers.

While we are in REM sleep, our brains are empty from noradrenaline, which is akin to adrenaline. It is an anxiety-producing molecule, and REM sleep is the only time of the day when this body chemical is not being produced. What we know is that REM sleep offers many benefits and here are two additional therapeutic ones:

- Remembering details of our experience and integrating them with our other thoughts.
- Forgetting the painful thoughts and memories that linger.

Another interesting study was done with these thoughts. A group of participants was shown pictures of both pleasant and traumatic events and their reactions were captured in an MRI scan. As before, the group was split, and half were sent home to sleep for the night, while the other half stayed and viewed the same images again after being awake between the two viewings. Guess what? Those that had slept had a significantly reduced emotional reaction to the images the next morning.

The question remains: is REM sleep what we need to accomplish this therapy or is it the dreaming event that helps us through the trauma? By following participants lives over a period of years, those who reported dreaming about the events that created mental health issues like depression, had full recoveries, while the ones who had no dreams still suffered from their mental health condition. Evidence that the dreams are just as important to our well being as REM sleep. PTSD patients have reported similar positive responses regarding their war experiences and recovery from the trauma. Another important finding, particularly for people living with PTSD was the fact that lowering their noradrenaline levels during sleep may be helpful.

Dr. Murray Raskind, a Veteran's Hospital doctor, began treating some of his patients with prazosin, a generic drug intended to lower blood pressure. An exciting side effect was revealed when these PTSD patients reported that since taking the drug their recurring nightmares had completely halted. They felt less afraid and were better able to fall asleep at night. Prazosin was lowering noradrenaline in these patients and allowing them to have a higher quality of REM sleep that reduced nightmares. What a fabulous finding!

Still another finding from the studies was that participants who were deprived of REM sleep were not able to discern facial expressions that displayed someone's mood. Imagine the impact to the world from a social perspective if we didn't have that ability. After quality RFM sleep, participants had excellent social comprehension the following day.

Chapter Eleven

You may recall that Paul McCartney, Beetle extraordinaire, wrote at least two of their hits based on his dreams. Both *Yesterday* and *Let It Be* came from Paul's dreaming mind when he woke up with the tunes in his head. He headed for the piano, and the rest is musical history. Rolling Stone's, Keith Richards slept with a guitar and a tape recorder by his bed to record his nighttime ideas and the opening riff to *Satisfaction* is one of his results. Shelley's *Frankenstein* also came from a dream.

Based on this unscientific information, our author proceeded with another test using anagrams with participants. Test subjects were shown several anagram puzzles (OSEOG = GOOSE) and asked to solve the problems. Then they could sleep, but were awakened four times during the night, twice while in NREM sleep and twice in REM sleep. Each was given several new anagrams to solve, and the result was that the participants were as much as 35 percent more successful when awakening from REM sleep than they were from either waking hours or NREM sleep. Another example was a test that involved seeing a chart of interconnecting ideas, a bit like a flowchart. When participants were awakened from NREM sleep, they remembered the chart and were quickly able to get their brains back into the interconnecting words; however, when they awoke from REM sleep, the connections were less linked, and their brains were remembering things in a whole different perspective, more creatively.

So, when you hear the term, "let's sleep on it" again, consider this: REM sleep allows for enhanced comprehension, NREM sleep allows for greater learning. A related test where participants were given mathematical problems to solve, revealed the same results. There was a shortcut method to solve each of the problems, and only those test subjects who could attain REM sleep identified the shortcut 60 percent of the time. The non-sleepers were challenged to identify the same shortcut.

Chapter Twelve

This chapter focuses on sleep disorders:

- Somnambulism is a disorder that involves movement like sleepwalking, talking, eating or texting as examples. Under this condition, the nervous system's activities spike from the very bottom to the very top; however, it gets stuck somewhere in between, and the body is trapped between wakefulness and deep sleep. In most cases, this is nothing to be overly concerned about, and it is common for both children and adults. There is one known very scary story associated with this disorder. The condensed very of the story is that a son in law (Mr. Parks), who had wonderful relationship with both of his wife's parents, awoke one night, got in his car (barefoot), drove to his in-law's home and killed his mother in law, with a knife he got from their kitchen, and attempted to kill his father in law. The gentleman had been under great stress from losing his job, and he had large gambling debts. Both items were contributors to his insomnia. After committing the acts, he got back in his car and at some point, while driving back home noticed the blood on his arms and hands. He drove to the police reporting that he thought he had killed someone. Jumping quickly to the result, Mr. Parks was found not guilty of the murder or attempted murder because he was asleep when it all happened. A bizarre and disturbing story; however, note that in most cases of somnambulism, intervention is not necessary and is a benign ailment.

Insomnia is officially defined as:

- An inadequate ability to sleep
- An adequate opportunity to sleep

And there are several aspects to the condition:

- Onset insomnia is trouble getting to sleep
- Maintenance insomnia is difficulty staying asleep
- Paradoxical insomnia is the illusion of poor sleep when it is really a form of hypochondria

To be diagnosed with insomnia the following conditions must be met:

- Challenging to fall asleep, stay asleep or early morning wake ups.
- Feeling noteworthy daytime distress or impairments.
- Occurs at least three nights per week for more than three consecutive months.
- No coexisting mental conditions that may cause insomnia.

About one in nine people are diagnosed with insomnia. That comes to about 40 million nationwide folks who struggle with sleep. Some of the triggers that have been associated with this disorder include:

- Environmental factors
- Age
- Too much light while sleeping
- Wrong room temperatures
- Caffeine, tobacco or alcohol consumption
- Emotional concerns, worry, distress

You will recall our sympathetic nervous system from earlier chapters. If it becomes overactive for a long period, that puts our fight or flight response in high alert, and it never turns off, which is unacceptable. It results in a higher core body temperature, increased cortisol, adrenaline, and noradrenaline, all of which raise our heart rate. An increased and altered pattern of brain activity is the result. In short, insomnia patients never get relief from worry or anxiety, and the brain never gets a needed break.

- Narcolepsy is a medical, neurological disorder that originates in our central nervous system. The three primary symptoms are:
- Excessive day sleepiness, or an inability to stay awake during the day.
- Sleep paralysis happens if you lose the ability to talk or move.
- Cataplexy is certainly the most disturbing symptom, as it involves seizures and a sudden loss of muscle control. These are often triggered by an extremely positive or negative emotion. News of death or an incredibly funny joke are two spectrum examples.

The disorder dictates that most narcoleptics lose all their emotional baggage, for obvious reasons. Our sleep/wake switch is in the center of our brains below the thalamus in the same region as our hypothalamus. The hypothalamus releases orexin, which is a neurotransmitter that triggers our awake or sleep clock. In nearly 90 percent of postmortem investigations, narcoleptic individuals had lost nearly 90 percent of their orexin producing cells. This means that they constantly lived in "no man's land" between wakefulness and sleep.

Treating narcolepsy is largely done via the use of amphetamines to improve awake time and antidepressants to help with sleep paralysis and cataplexy. While other treatments are being studied, for now, there isn't a lot of promise.

- Fatal familial insomnia (FFI) is a rare genetic disorder that offers no cures and no treatments. All diagnosed patients are dead in less than a year. We have been able to tie the disorder back to PrNP, a prion protein gene that attacks the thalamus and destroys it, resulting in an individual who can never get their needed sleep. So sad! Since the uncertainty of the disease is unknown from a genetics perspective, the question becomes: "would you want to know your fate and that of any potential offspring?" Another ethical conundrum.

You will see many, many reports of how much sleep we need or should have. Make note that there is the need for a defined amount of sleep and an opportunity to allow for sleep. These are two distinct thoughts. So, is there such a thing as too much sleep?

When we take things to extreme levels, yes it becomes unhealthy. The bottom line from the perspective of our author is that eight hours of sleep per night is an optimal number. Variations are going to occur based on how you feel if you've contracted the flu, etc.

Chapter Thirteen

A lot has changed over the last few decades, not to mention the last few centuries. Most notably the changes we have experienced that impact our sleep habits are:

- Electric light or LED lights (we no longer base our activities on the sun) and we tend to stay up later by two to three hours. Even the smallest light has been proven to delay our release of melatonin, which tells us its time to sleep. Even reading on a tablet produces enough light to decrease our melatonin levels by as much as 50 percent. The result of our technology:
- We've lost significant amounts of REM sleep.
- Test subjects admitted feeling less rested and sleepier during the day.
- Participants suffered about a 90-minute delay in their melatonin rise.

We know that maintaining complete darkness during sleep hours is critical.

- Standardized temperature control. Falling asleep in a room that is too cold, is much easier than falling sleep in a room that is too hot. Largely because the colder room is causing your brain and your body to lower their temperatures. The "perfect" bedroom temperature, according to our author is 65 to 70 degrees Fahrenheit. That is assuming, standard nighttime attire and adequate bedding.
- Many of us believe that the fabulous, hot nighttime bath helps us sleep. And it does; however, not the reasons you may think. Rather than faster sleep because we're all warm and toasty, the hot bath caused our blood to draw closer to the surface of our skin, so when we rise from the bath, our core body temperature drops and that is what helps us fall asleep more quickly. This will result in about 15 percent deeper NREM sleep.
- Caffeine.

- ○ Alcohol is one of the most powerful blockers of REM sleep, consider skipping that nightcap.
- ○ Punching a time clock daily has caused all of us to be forced awake, and it began with those clocks in factories where workers had to punch in by a certain, defined time. Alarm clocks and other means of ensuring we wake up in time to get to school or work forces us to end sleep unnaturally. That causes our nervous system to jump into overdrive, alert our fight or flight response, up to our heart rate and create a spike in our blood pressure.
- ○ Reaching and maintaining an acceptable sleep and wake schedule is highly recommended to avoid those jolts to our bodies and brains. We all know that can be easier said than done.

Chapter Fourteen

As for sleeping pills, about ten million of us have tried the sleep aids. They are unnatural, can be damaging to our health, and increase our risk of life-threatening diseases. Foremost, they do not result in a natural sleep; they simply act as sedatives. Some of the undesirable side effects include: sleepiness the following day, forgetfulness, partial amnesia and they can also create an unintended vicious cycle. Studies have indicated that pills, either over the counter or prescription only produce "minor" improvements in our sleep. One study, which involved 20,000 subjects, half of whom were taking some form of sleeping aid and the remaining half, not taking anything resulted in an increased mortality rate that was 4.6 times greater for the pill poppers. They were tracked over a two and one-half year period. Alarmingly, those who took a mere 18 pills per year, were still 3.6 times more likely to die. Contributors to the earlier deaths were:

- An increased chance of infection from unnatural sleep.
- An increased risk of a fatal car accident.
- Cancer, because pill users were 60 percent more likely to develop cancer.
- We are not saying that sleeping aids cause cancer, we are stating that it can be a contributor.

Rather than being drawn to drug-induced sleep, the medical industry currently supports cognitive behavioral therapy (CBT). By working with a therapist, patients received tips for breaking bad sleep habits. Things like:

- Reducing alcohol and caffeine intake.
- Removing technology from the bedroom (that includes phones, tablets, televisions, gaming systems).
- Establishing a regular bed and wake up time.
- Avoid falling asleep on the couch and go to bed only when you feel sleepy.
- Don't lie in bed too long awake, get up and do something relaxing until you feel sleepy.

- ○ Reduce anxiousness, try to mentally "check out" before bedtime.
- ○ Remove clocks from easy sight to avoid being a clock watcher.

Next steps may include limiting patients to only six hours of sleep for a while until they fall asleep more readily and sleep more soundly. This method is proving itself to be the "prescription" of choice.

Physical activity is another method to enhance sleep habits; however, it is not recommended right before bedtime. This is because it will make it harder to reduce your core temperature to initiate sleep.

Eating also has a sleep impact. High carb, low-fat diets will increase REM sleep, but decrease NREM sleep. High sugar and other carbs, and low fiber result in reduced NREM sleep and more nighttime wakeups.

Chapter Fifteen

Sleep impacts all our lives as well as all aspects of our lives. For example:

- o Sleep deprivation impacts the ability to think and function well at work. In fact, studies show that inadequate sleep can cost as much as $2,000 per employee. Employees lacking sleep are less happy, motivated, productive, creative and lazier. Also, they also tend to be less ethical and more deviant. Companies like Nike, Google, and NASA, have already learned this and responded accordingly by allowing their staffs to work schedules that better match their circadian rhythms.
- o Think of our military and that of other governments. Torture by way of sleep deprivation has been used widely, to "break" prisoners or hostages into spilling bits of information. This type of torture violates both our eighth and fourteenth amendments as cruel and unusual punishment.
- o In the field of education, some schools begin their day before 7:30 am, which causes students to rise as early as 5:30 am. This can have an adverse impact on moods and learning abilities. Schools that have adopted later start times are reaping benefits like decreased behavioral problems, better attendance, and less substance abuse. Another benefit of later start times is later finished times, which keeps the kids busy and out of trouble until parents can get home from work. So, again, less opportunity for mischief. The leading cause of death among teenagers is traffic accidents. Since inadequate sleep time impacts that, the later school start times add to the life expectancy of our children.
- o Doctors and nurses and other healthcare professional work incredibly long hours, which sets the stage for sleep-deprived healthcare workers. Not good for them or us, as patients. You can imagine the adverse impacts of sleep

deprivation on surgeons, residents and others who are known to work long shifts. A lack of sleep opportunities can also lead them to look for substances they think may be helpful, cocaine for example. Not to mention driving and being far too drowsy to operate a vehicle.

Remember the Exxon Valdez? At first the captain was accused of being drunk; however, the fact was that he turned over command to his third mate, who had only had six of the prior 48 hours of sleep. The ecosystem still hasn't recovered from ten to 40 million gallons of oil that impacted over 1,200 miles of shoreline, cost the lives of more than half a million seabirds, 5,000 otters, 300 seals, 200 bald eagles, and 20 orca whales.

Chapter Sixteen

How can we deal with our epidemic of sleeplessness?

- We can teach home heating/cooling technologies to set proper sleep temperatures.
- Further, set temperature controls to respond to our body's expectations for temperatures rather than a single constant temperature.
- Train our home lighting efforts to gradually decrease daily as the day advances to night. Create new bulbs in colors that are less damaging to melatonin production.
- Develop devices that can detect our sleep quality and adjust our alarm clocks/work times to better meet our bodies needs for NREM and REM sleep.
- Create work environment lighting that adjusts to the needs of the individual.
- Provide better sleep education to the world, so as individuals, we can take better care of our needs.
- With our wearable technology, add in features that allow users to know their vital medical records at any time during the day so that they can react appropriately.
- Add better sleep tracking mechanisms to our wearable technology to detect REM versus NREM sleep.
- Add analytics to the mechanisms that provide suggestive activities for improvement.
- Establish medical practices that put more focus on sleep and how it is impacting our health, treat the whole person, not just a disease or a symptom.

Yes, much of our sleep challenges are cultural and won't likely be addressed by a small group of individuals; however, if communities, schools, corporations, and governments join forces to meet the goal of creating better sleep education and environments, we could begin the transition to a more informed, sleep fulfilled culture.

Discussion Questions

Why We Sleep: Unlocking the Power of Sleep and Dreams

- Discuss the difference between REM and NREM sleep.
- What are the benefits of both REM and NREM sleep.
- Discuss the adverse impacts of sleep deprevation.
- Discuss the types of sleep disorders.
- What aspects of our health are impacted by sleep, or a lack of sleep?
- Do dreams offer us any value?
- Discuss how technology has changed our sleep culture.
- What ideas do you have to address our sleep deprived societies?
- What is the best method to begin an educational effort to get our kids on a better sleep track and inform the public of the virtues of eight hours of nightly sleep?
- What role, if any, do you think healthcare professionals play today in addressing sleep ailments? Discuss how you feel that should or should not change.

Publication/Author Information

Why We Sleep: Unlocking the Power of Sleep and Dreams

Dr. Walker is currently a neuroscience professor at UC Berkeley and director of its Sleep and Neuroimaging Lab. Before that role, he taught psychiatry at Harvard University. Although *Why We Sleep* is his first book, he has numerous scientific study publications and has been a guest on *Nova*, *BBC News*, and *60 Minutes*.

Dr. Walker is also a Sleep Scientist at Google, Sleep Scientist, and Public Sleep Advocate. He also has a website, which can found at https://www.sleepdiplomat.com/.

Dr. Walker earned his degree in neuroscience from Nottingham University, UK, and his Ph.D. in neurophysiology from the Medical Research Council, London, UK. Dedicated to the communication of science, Dr. Walker is an internationally recognized speaker, media discussant, and frequent feature on mainstream television and radio outlets, including *CBS with Charlie Rose*, and the *BBC*.

Dr. Walker holds numerous US patents concerning consumer-based sleep recording, sleep tracking and sleep stimulation. Dr. Walker also owns several patents focused on the commercial use of consumer-based sleep measures as they apply to health, technology, business, and enterprise. Previously, Dr. Walker has served as scientific counsel for numerous technology companies, including Hello and Fitbit.

THANK YOU!

Brief Books pledges to always do our very best to produce high quality and entertaining books for you to enjoy. With that being said - the opinions, comments, criticisms, and compliments that we receive from fellow readers are always being taken to heart.

Take part to keep us going, add your review on Amazon and tell us and others what you think!

You can leave a review here!

Thanks once again.

Sincerely,

Brief Books